New Mum Affirmations

to build confidence and support maternal mental health

Keeping Mum Press, 2022

Matrescence (n)

**The transformative transition to motherhood.
This is a time of growth, pain, discomfort and exploration.**

Becoming a mother is a magical time of life, but it can also present some challenges, as new mums have to quickly adapt to caring for their newborn 24/7, get used to to their own changing bodies and hormones, and try to discover a new sense of self as a mother.

Around 1 in 5 women will experience a perinatal mental health problem in pregnancy or the early postnatal years, ranging from stress and anxiety to postnatal depression, PTSD and postpartum psychosis.

Meanwhile, many others will struggle with low confidence - perhaps in their parenting abilities or with their body image since having a baby - with studies revealing that 70% will hide or underplay their illness.

However, there are many tools available to help, and positive affirmations can be just one way to help new mothers adopt a positive mindset and build confidence. In this book, you will find 30 affirmations for new mums to read and repeat whenever you need a little boost, or a reminder of what a great job you are doing.

There are five blank pages for you to write down more of your favourite quotes, set goals, or even add photos of you and your baby!

Lastly, you will find resources for perinatal mental health support, from expert organisations including PANDAs and the Maternal Mental Health Alliance.

Always remember, you are an amazing mother, and you are doing a great job.

I am exactly the mother my baby needs

My baby is not giving me a hard time, my baby is having a hard time

I am doing a great job and I am learning every day

I trust my intuition to show me the way

It is not selfish to take time for myself

I am allowed to ask for help

It's okay not to enjoy every moment

I look for the good in everyday things

Nobody knows my baby better than me

One bad day does not make me a bad mum

I am doing an amazing job

My baby and I are learning together

My baby doesn't want a perfect mum

I am enough

I aim for progress, not perfection

I am doing my best and that is enough

I am not alone

My baby loves me no matter what

I allow myself to enjoy this precious time with my baby

I will not compare myself to others

I am proud of my body and what it has achieved

My body continues to heal every day

I am surrounded by those who love, support and respect me

I am making the best choices for my baby

I take care of my own needs too

My baby and I have a sacred bond

I am strong and capable

I welcome the challenges of motherhood with gratitude

I am a dedicated and loving mother

I feel the love of others around me

Resources for Maternal Mental Health Advice and Support

PANDAS Foundation
pandasfoundation.org.uk

Maternal Mental Health Alliance
maternalmentalhealthalliance.org

Birth Better
makebirthbetter.org

Home Start
home-start.org.uk

MumsAid
mums-aid.org

The Birth Trauma Association
birthtraumaassociation.org.uk

Printed in Great Britain
by Amazon